Principles of Software Engineering:

A Comprehensive Guide to Development, Testing, and Documentation.

By

Michael Andrew Lambert Jr

Abstract

This book, "**Principles of Software Engineering: A Comprehensive Guide to Development, Testing, and Documentation,**" provides an in-depth exploration of the foundational concepts and practices in software engineering. Spanning nine chapters, it addresses key topics such as design patterns, software reengineering, and the importance of effective documentation. Each chapter builds upon the last, presenting theoretical frameworks alongside practical applications to enhance understanding and implementation in real-world scenarios.

Beginning with an introduction to the Unified Modeling Language (UML) and design principles, the book transitions into discussions on modularization and software testing fundamentals. It delves into the complexities of legacy systems, highlighting strategies for reverse engineering and the importance of updating software for modern platforms. The significance of thorough documentation is emphasized, balancing clarity and detail to ensure usability for both developers and end-users.

Reflecting on critical design patterns and information security, the book equips readers with the tools needed to create maintainable and secure software solutions. Through continuous self-assessment and reflection, the content aims to foster a deeper understanding of the nuances of software engineering, encouraging readers to apply these principles in their own development projects. This comprehensive guide serves as a valuable resource for students, practitioners, and anyone interested in mastering the art and science of software engineering.

Table of Contents

Ch 1: The Foundations of Software 9

Ch 2: Software Requirements and Architecture 15

Ch 3: Use Cases and Scenarios 23

Ch 4: Understanding System Context 27

Ch 5: Unit Testing and Test Case Design 37

Ch 6: Software Estimation and Measurement 47

Ch 7: Analysis of Design Approaches in Systems 57

Ch 8: Software Reengineering and Documentation 67

Ch 9: Conclusion and Future Directions 77

References 83

Chapter One: The Foundations of Software Engineering

In the evolving landscape of technology, software engineering stands as a cornerstone of modern development practices. The Software Development Life Cycle (SDLC) is a crucial framework that guides the process of software creation, encompassing various stages from initial concept to deployment and maintenance.

Understanding the Software Development Life Cycle

The SDLC provides a structured approach to software development, allowing teams to navigate the complexities involved in creating software solutions. It consists of several phases, including requirements gathering, design, implementation, testing, deployment, and maintenance. Each phase plays a vital role in ensuring that the final product meets user needs and quality standards.

Software Development Models

Different software development models are applied within the SDLC framework, each suited to specific project requirements and environments. Among the most prominent are:

1. **Waterfall Model**: This linear approach progresses through distinct phases sequentially. While it offers clarity and structure, it can be inflexible in adapting to changes once a phase is completed.

2. **Incremental Model**: This model breaks the project into smaller, manageable segments or increments, allowing for partial implementations and early user feedback. It promotes flexibility and risk management.

3. **Agile Model**: Emphasizing collaboration and adaptability, Agile methodologies allow teams to

respond to changing requirements throughout the development process. This iterative approach supports continuous improvement and client engagement.

The Importance of Software Engineering

Software engineering is critical for developing reliable, scalable, and efficient software systems. As technology advances, the complexity of software projects increases, leading to what are often termed "wicked problems." These challenges require innovative solutions and an understanding of both technical and non-technical factors affecting software development.

A significant factor in the successful delivery of software lies in choosing the appropriate development model. For instance, Agile methodologies have gained prominence in large, complex projects, as they provide the flexibility needed to manage evolving requirements while ensuring a structured approach to development.

Historical Context and Progress

The history of software engineering reveals a field that has matured significantly since its inception. In the early days of computing, software development was an experimental and often chaotic process. The first iterations of software tools were built with limited resources, and the methodologies we now take for granted were still being formulated.

For example, when Microsoft released its first word processor in 1989, it faced numerous challenges. The development team operated with the constraints of the era, utilizing lower-level programming languages like assembly or early versions of C. This starkly contrasts with today's environment, where high-level languages such as Python offer developers enhanced capabilities and productivity.

The comparison between software development and other engineering fields, like aerospace and civil engineering, underscores the relative infancy of software engineering. By the time personal computing became mainstream, fields like bridge and aircraft construction had long histories and established methodologies. For instance, during World War II, aircraft had already been in use for decades, showcasing a depth of experience that software engineering was still striving to achieve.

Conclusion

In summary, the foundations of software engineering and the SDLC highlight the critical role that structured methodologies play in the development of software. Understanding the various models available—such as Waterfall, Incremental, and Agile—equips engineers to navigate the complexities of their projects more effectively. As technology continues to evolve, so too will the practices and approaches that define software engineering, making it an ever-relevant field in our digital age.

Chapter Two: Software Requirements and Architecture

The success of any software project hinges on a clear understanding of software requirements and a well-defined architecture. These foundational elements not only shape the development process but also ensure that the final product aligns with user needs and business objectives.

Requirements Elicitation

Requirements elicitation is a critical phase in the software development process. Users possess valuable insights into business processes, rules, and specific needs that are essential for defining what a system must achieve. Their practical experience allows them to articulate requirements that are closely aligned with business goals. However, users often encounter challenges in effectively communicating their needs, particularly due to their varying levels of technical understanding. This communication gap can lead to misunderstandings, making it difficult to create precise and actionable specifications.

Conversely, developers bring technical expertise and problem-solving skills to the table. They transform user requirements into practical software solutions while anticipating potential technical obstacles. This ability to break down requirements into manageable tasks is crucial for effective planning and execution. Nonetheless, developers may struggle to grasp the non-technical language used by users, which can lead to misinterpretations. Additionally, there can be a tendency among developers to prioritize technical considerations over user experience, resulting in systems that are technically sound but not entirely user-centric.

The Importance of Collaboration

Collaboration between users and developers is vital for effective requirements elicitation. Users contribute insights based on their knowledge and practical experience, while developers provide the technical expertise necessary to create viable solutions. By acknowledging the limitations of both groups and bridging the communication gap, the requirements elicitation process can be significantly enhanced. This collaborative approach is essential for developing software solutions that meet user needs and align with technical feasibility.

Defining Requirements

In software development, requirements are typically categorized into functional and non-functional requirements.

- **Functional Requirements** define what the system should do. They describe specific behaviors or functions, such as processing user inputs or generating reports.

- **Non-Functional Requirements** refer to how the system performs certain functions. These may include usability, performance, reliability, and security considerations.

Verifiability of Requirements

A critical aspect of requirements engineering is ensuring that requirements are verifiable. For example, consider the following requirements:

1. **User-Friendliness**: "The user interface must be user-friendly and easy to use."

    - This requirement is subjective and challenging to measure, making it difficult to test. User feedback through usability tests can help gauge this aspect.

2. **Navigation Efficiency**: "The number of mouse clicks required to navigate to any window must be less than 10."

    o   This requirement is specific and quantifiable, allowing for straightforward validation through navigation tests.

3. **Simplicity of Use**: "The user interface must be simple enough for any user to operate with minimal training."

    o   While somewhat subjective, this requirement can be assessed through training tests that measure user performance after a brief training session.

4. **Latency**: "The maximum latency from the moment a user clicks a hyperlink until the new page starts rendering must be 1 second over a broadband connection."

- This is a clear and measurable requirement, verifiable through performance testing.

5. **Data Recovery**: "In case of failure, the system must facilitate easy recovery with minimal loss of important data."

    - This requirement can be challenging to quantify, but it can be evaluated through recovery tests that monitor the time taken and the extent of data loss.

Software Architecture

Software architecture plays a pivotal role in determining the overall design and structure of a system. It encompasses the high-level organization of software components, their interactions, and the principles guiding the design. A well-defined architecture can greatly influence the system's scalability, maintainability, and performance.

Different architectural patterns and styles, such as layered architecture, microservices, and event-driven architectures, provide frameworks for structuring applications effectively. Understanding these patterns is crucial for designing robust systems that can adapt to changing requirements and technologies.

Conclusion

In conclusion, the foundations of software requirements and architecture are vital for the success of any software project. Effective requirements elicitation, characterized by collaboration between users and developers, leads to clear, actionable specifications. Additionally, understanding and implementing appropriate software architecture ensures that systems are designed to meet both functional and non-functional requirements. As the field of software engineering continues to evolve, mastering these principles will remain essential for delivering high-quality software solutions that align with user needs and business goals.

Chapter 3: Use Cases and Scenarios in Software Development

In software development and requirements analysis, use cases and scenarios play pivotal but distinct roles, helping teams understand user interactions with systems and the specific functionalities required.

Use Cases

A **use case** provides a comprehensive overview of how users interact with a system to achieve specific objectives. It outlines the sequence of actions taken by users and the system's corresponding responses. Use cases are essential for documenting functional requirements and are typically represented in diagram form using Unified Modeling Language (UML). For example, in an online shopping platform, a use case titled "Place Order" illustrates how a customer selects items, adds them to a cart, and completes the transaction (Bell, 2003).

Use cases help define the system's functionality and encompass all potential user interactions. They are particularly useful for documenting broad requirements and understanding the system's overall scope.

Scenarios

A **scenario** represents a specific sequence of actions and interactions between users and the system to achieve a particular goal within a use case. Scenarios provide a focused perspective, highlighting a single path or flow of events. They help illustrate how the system operates under specific conditions or inputs. For instance, within the "Place Order" use case, a scenario might detail the process where a customer adds items to the cart, applies a discount code, and selects express shipping (Ambler, 2003-2018).

Scenarios are critical for examining particular paths or situations in a use case. They aid in describing interactions, confirming system behavior, and understanding specific user requirements or exceptional cases.

Examples

Use Case Example

Consider the process of booking a flight online. This use case would encompass several steps, such as selecting travel dates, choosing a flight, entering passenger information, and completing the payment process (Bell, 2004).

Scenario Example

Within the "Booking a Flight" use case, a scenario could involve a user who needs to make changes to their booking after receiving the initial confirmation. This might include adjusting travel dates or upgrading seating preferences (Ambler, 2003-2018).

Conclusion

Ultimately, use cases provide a high-level view of system functionality, while scenarios delve into the specifics of user interactions within those functions. Both constructs are integral to effective requirements elicitation and software design, ensuring that user needs are met and that systems function as intended.

Chapter 4: Understanding System Context and Responsibility Assignment in Software Development

In software development, grasping the environment in which a system operates is crucial. The system's context provides a holistic view of how it interacts with users, other systems, and external factors. Understanding this context is vital for several reasons.

Defining Boundaries and Interfaces

Modeling the system context helps establish clear boundaries and interfaces. This clarity ensures a comprehensive understanding of the system's scope, effectively preventing scope creep and identifying essential interfaces for communication with other systems or components.

Identifying Stakeholder Needs

By analyzing the system context, engineers can discern the needs and expectations of various stakeholders, including end-users, business owners, and external partners. This understanding is critical for ensuring that the system meets its intended requirements and delivers value to its users.

Mitigating Risks and Ensuring Compatibility

Understanding the system context allows for early identification of potential risks and compatibility issues. By comprehending how the system will interact with its environment, engineers can design robust and flexible solutions that adapt to external influences.

Errors Without System Context Modeling

Misalignment with User Requirements

Without a thorough understanding of the system context, engineers risk creating a system that does not align with user needs. For instance, a mobile banking app designed without considering limited internet access in remote areas may rely too heavily on real-time data synchronization, leading to poor performance and user dissatisfaction. Contextual awareness enables engineers to address such limitations, possibly by incorporating offline capabilities.

Integration Failures with External Systems

Neglecting to model system context can lead to integration failures with external systems. For example, an e-commerce platform developed without accounting for payment gateways, shipping services, and inventory management systems may overlook critical details such as API compatibility and communication protocols. This oversight could result in transaction failures, inaccurate inventory updates, and delayed shipping notifications. Accurate context modeling ensures seamless interactions with external systems.

In summary, modeling the context of a system is essential for defining clear boundaries, understanding stakeholder needs, and mitigating risks. This practice guarantees that the developed system meets user requirements and integrates effectively with other systems. Failure to model the system context can result in software solutions that fall short of user needs and encounter integration challenges. Therefore, thorough context modeling is indispensable in the software development process.

GRASP Patterns in Responsibility Assignment

Understanding General Responsibility Assignment Software Patterns (GRASP) is essential in software design as these patterns provide a framework for assigning responsibilities efficiently to classes and objects. By adhering to these principles, software engineers can achieve low coupling and high cohesion, which enhance the maintainability and flexibility of software systems.

Key GRASP Patterns

One notable GRASP pattern is the **Information Expert**. This pattern suggests delegating responsibilities to the class that possesses the most relevant information to perform a task. For example, in a banking system, the **Customer** class would manage methods related to account management and transactions because it directly interacts with that data.

Another significant principle is **High Cohesion**, which organizes related functions within a specific class. This approach simplifies the system and enhances design clarity. For instance, a **FileHandler** class that includes methods for reading, writing, and closing files exemplifies high cohesion due to the close relationship among these operations.

Low Coupling is also critical, as it reduces the interdependencies between classes, promoting reusability and simplifying maintenance. The **Creator** pattern embodies this concept by suggesting that classes responsible for creating objects should have the necessary knowledge for their instantiation, thereby decreasing the dependency between the creator and the created objects.

In conclusion, GRASP patterns offer a systematic approach to assigning responsibilities in software design. By following principles like Information Expert, High Cohesion, and Low Coupling, software clarity and maintainability improve, while fostering effective collaboration between classes.

Concepts of Coupling and Cohesion

Coupling refers to the degree of reliance between classes or modules in a system, while cohesion measures how well the components within a module fit together. These concepts are crucial for creating reliable and manageable software systems.

Example of Coupling and Cohesion

Consider a **Library Management System** with classes such as **Book**, **Member**, and **Loan**.

- **Coupling Example**: If the **Book** class directly accesses the **Member** class to check out a book, this results in high coupling. The strong connection diminishes the system's adaptability to changes in either class.

- **Cohesion Example**: The **Loan** class exhibits high cohesion by containing methods like `calculateFine()`, `renewLoan()`, and `printLoanDetails()`, all focused on managing loans. These methods collaborate closely to achieve the common goal of loan management.

Ideal Combination of Coupling and Cohesion

Optimal software design comprises high cohesion and low coupling, where modules are well-organized with minimal interdependencies. This structure enhances reusability, simplifies maintenance, and improves system scalability.

Reasoning

High cohesion means classes are dedicated to specific tasks, leading to more organized and comprehensible code. For instance, a **PaymentProcessor** class that solely handles payment-related functions demonstrates high cohesion.

Low coupling minimizes the ripple effect of changes; adjustments in one module are less likely to affect others. For example, if the **PaymentProcessor** class interacts with a **PaymentGateway** class through an interface, modifications in the gateway will not disrupt the processor, showcasing the benefits of low coupling.

Supporting evidence from Aldrich and Garrod (2015) emphasizes that high cohesion and low coupling are fundamental principles in object-oriented design, contributing to software that is easier to understand, maintain, and extend.

In summary, achieving high cohesion and low coupling in software design ensures robustness and flexibility, aligning with industry best practices and enhancing overall software quality.

Chapter 5: Unit Testing and Test Case Design

Unit testing is a critical component of software development that ensures the quality and reliability of software systems. In this chapter, we will explore essential test case design methods and their applications, emphasizing the importance of a structured approach to testing. By focusing on three primary methods—Equivalence Partitioning, Boundary Value Analysis, and Decision Table Testing—we will illustrate how these techniques can improve the effectiveness of unit testing.

5.1 Importance of Test Case Design Methods

Choosing the right test case design methods is vital for achieving high-quality software. Effective testing can uncover potential defects, validate functionality, and ensure that the software meets user requirements. The following sections detail three key test case design methods that are particularly effective in unit testing.

5.1.1 Equivalence Partitioning

Equivalence Partitioning is a technique that divides input data into distinct partitions, where each partition is expected to yield similar results. This method reduces the number of test cases needed by allowing testers to focus on representative values from each partition instead of testing every possible scenario.

Example Application: Consider a program designed to classify triangles based on their side lengths. The inputs can be categorized into two main partitions: valid triangles and invalid triangles. Valid triangles adhere to the triangle inequality theorem, while invalid triangles do not. By selecting key values from each partition—for example, testing sides that form valid triangles (3, 4, 5) and invalid triangles (1, 2, 3)—we can effectively validate the program's functionality while minimizing redundant tests.

5.1.2 Boundary Value Analysis

Boundary Value Analysis focuses on testing values at the edges of input ranges, where errors are most likely to occur. This technique is particularly useful for identifying off-by-one errors and issues related to boundary conditions.

Example Application: Applying Boundary Value Analysis to the triangle classification problem involves testing the minimum and maximum allowable side lengths. For instance, testing side lengths of (1, 1, 1) verifies the smallest possible valid triangle, while testing (0, 1, 1) checks the behavior when inputs are at the boundary of validity. By emphasizing edge cases, this method helps ensure that the software accurately handles inputs that lie at critical thresholds.

5.1.3 Decision Table Testing

Decision Table Testing is a systematic method that organizes input combinations and expected results into a table format. This approach ensures that all potential combinations of inputs are accounted for, making it easier to validate complex logic.

Example Application: In the triangle classification scenario, a decision table can be constructed to outline various combinations of side lengths and their corresponding classifications. The table can specify conditions for scalene, isosceles, and equilateral triangles, as well as invalid triangles. For instance, if the input sides are $(5, 5, 8)$, the table would indicate that the output should be "Isosceles." This comprehensive method ensures that the software correctly identifies triangle types under various scenarios.

5.2 Test Cases for Triangle Classification

To illustrate the application of the discussed test case design methods, we will develop specific test cases for a triangle classification program.

5.2.1 Test Cases

- **Test Case 1**: Equilateral Triangle

  Input: (3, 3, 3)

  Expected Output: "Equilateral"

  Reason: All sides are equal; thus, the triangle is equilateral.

- **Test Case 2**: Isosceles Triangle (Two sides equal)

  Input: (5, 5, 8)

  Expected Output: "Isosceles"

  Reason: Two sides are equal; thus, the triangle is isosceles.

- **Test Case 3**: Scalene Triangle (All sides different)

  Input: (4, 5, 6)

Expected Output: "Scalene"

Reason: All sides are different; thus, the triangle is scalene.

- **Test Case 4**: Not a Triangle (Sum of two sides not greater than the third)

  Input: (1, 2, 3)

  Expected Output: "Not a Triangle"

  Reason: The sum of two sides is not greater than the third side; thus, these lengths do not form a triangle.

- **Test Case 5**: Isosceles Triangle (Another example)

  Input: (7, 7, 10)

  Expected Output: "Isosceles"

  Reason: Two sides are equal; thus, the triangle is isosceles.

- **Test Case 6**: Scalene Triangle (Another example)

  Input: (8, 9, 10)

Expected Output: "Scalene"

Reason: All sides are different; thus, the triangle is scalene.

5.2.2 Additional Considerations

- **Edge Case**: Ensure the program correctly handles the smallest possible input values that form a triangle, such as (1, 1, 1).

- **Error Handling**: Test the program's response to invalid inputs, including negative numbers and zero.

5.3 Reflective Statement

This unit emphasized the importance of a systematic approach to software testing. Engaging with the course material provided a deeper understanding of test-driven implementation and the various aspects of software testing. Key topics included the significance of test case design methods, the structure of effective unit tests, and the concepts of test coverage and code refactoring.

By applying these methods, I have gained valuable insights into ensuring software reliability and quality. The skills developed in this unit will significantly benefit my future endeavors in software development, enabling me to create more robust and maintainable code. A key lesson learned is the value of adopting a methodical approach to testing, which not only enhances code quality but also reduces the likelihood of defects.

5.4 Conclusion

In conclusion, effective unit testing is paramount in delivering high-quality software. By employing techniques such as Equivalence Partitioning, Boundary Value Analysis, and Decision Table Testing, developers can ensure thorough testing of software components. As software systems continue to grow in complexity, the importance of well-structured testing strategies will only increase, making these principles essential for successful software development.

Chapter 6: Software Estimation and Measurement

In the realm of software engineering, understanding and measuring software complexity is vital for ensuring quality and maintainability. This chapter delves into the intricacies of cyclomatic complexity and its relationship with software attributes such as maintainability and readability. We will explore the challenges of validating these relationships, discuss measurement theory, and apply these concepts through practical examples, particularly focusing on the quicksort algorithm.

6.1 Understanding Cyclomatic Complexity

Cyclomatic complexity, introduced by Thomas McCabe in 1976, serves as a quantitative measure of a program's complexity based on its control flow. Specifically, it quantifies the number of linearly independent paths through a program's source code, providing insight into the structural complexity of the software (McCabe, 1976). The formula for calculating cyclomatic complexity V(G) is:

$$V(G)=E-N+2P$$

where E represents the number of edges, N denotes the number of nodes, and P is the number of connected components. This metric not only aids in assessing the complexity of individual functions but also informs broader implications for software maintainability.

6.1.1 Example Application: Quicksort Algorithm

To illustrate cyclomatic complexity, we can analyze the quicksort algorithm, a widely used sorting technique known for its efficiency. By constructing a flowchart for the quicksort procedure, we can visualize its control flow and compute its cyclomatic complexity.

Flowchart Analysis: The flowchart for quicksort depicts various paths the algorithm can take based on input conditions. For instance, the algorithm may diverge into recursive calls based on pivot selection and partitioning criteria.

Cyclomatic Complexity Calculation:

- **Edges**: The edges (e1 through e8) represent the flow of control between different nodes in the algorithm.
- **Nodes**: The nodes correspond to decision points and actions within the algorithm.

For the quicksort algorithm, using the aforementioned formula yields:

$$V(G) = 8 - 9 + 2 = 1$$

This result indicates a relatively simple and linear control flow. However, it's essential to note that this calculation only addresses the main procedure without accounting for recursive calls, which could significantly increase the overall cyclomatic complexity.

6.2 Challenges in Validating Relationships Between Internal and External Attributes

Validating the relationships between internal product attributes, such as cyclomatic complexity, and external attributes like maintainability is fraught with challenges.

6.2.1 Quantitative vs. Qualitative Metrics

One significant challenge lies in the distinction between quantitative and qualitative metrics. Cyclomatic complexity provides a clear, numerical measure of structural complexity, but it fails to encompass critical qualitative aspects of software, such as code readability, documentation quality, and adherence to coding standards (Sommerville, 2004). These qualitative factors significantly impact maintainability, making it difficult to draw direct correlations between internal metrics and external attributes.

6.2.2 Context-Dependent Relationships

The relationship between internal and external attributes is often context-dependent, varying across different software projects and development practices. For instance, a project with high cyclomatic complexity might still maintain excellent readability and documentation, leading to a high level of maintainability. Conversely, a project with lower complexity could be poorly documented and difficult to understand, resulting in decreased maintainability.

6.2.3 Psychological Complexity

Adding another layer of complexity is the notion of psychological complexity—the cognitive effort required by developers to understand and modify the code. This subjective measure can vary significantly among individuals, complicating the task of standardizing and correlating it with objective internal metrics like cyclomatic complexity. The intricacies of psychological complexity emphasize the need for a comprehensive approach to software measurement that integrates both quantitative and qualitative dimensions.

6.3 Insights from Learning Journal VI

Reflecting on my experiences from this unit, I developed a deeper understanding of measurement theory, module cohesion, coupling, and complexities such as cyclomatic and psychological complexity. My programming assignment required me to create a flowchart for the quicksort algorithm and calculate its cyclomatic complexity, reinforcing my grasp of these concepts and their practical applications.

6.3.1 Application to Professional and Academic Endeavors

The knowledge gained from this unit has direct applications in various aspects of my professional and academic journey:

- **Software Development**: Understanding cyclomatic complexity equips me to write more maintainable code by identifying potential areas of high complexity that might require refactoring.

- **Project Management**: Familiarity with effort estimation will enhance my ability to accurately estimate project durations and budgets, essential for effective project planning.

- **Code Review**: Insights into cohesion and coupling will facilitate thorough and effective code reviews, ensuring better software design and architecture.

6.3.2 The Balance of Internal and External Attributes

One crucial takeaway from this unit is the importance of balancing internal and external software attributes. While metrics like cyclomatic complexity offer quantifiable insights into code quality, it is equally vital to consider external factors such as maintainability, readability, and usability. Striking this balance is essential for developing software that is not only technically robust but also user-friendly and sustainable in the long term.

6.4 Conclusion

In conclusion, the exploration of software estimation and measurement, particularly through the lens of cyclomatic complexity, underscores the intricate relationships between internal and external software attributes. By integrating quantitative metrics with qualitative assessments and acknowledging the context-dependent nature of these relationships, software engineers can enhance the quality and maintainability of their code. As the field of software engineering continues to evolve, adopting a holistic approach that considers both technical and user-oriented aspects will be crucial for achieving successful outcomes in software development.

Chapter 7: Analysis of Design Approaches in ATM Systems

Introduction

In software engineering, the design of a system significantly impacts its functionality, maintainability, and overall user experience. This chapter focuses on the design considerations for an ATM system, specifically examining the "Withdraw Cash" scenario. The key components involved in this process include CustomerID, IDChecker, CustomerIDStorage, AcctInfo, AcctManager, and CashDispenserCtrl. A pivotal discussion arises around the potential merging of AcctInfo and AcctManager into a single Account object, prompting an analysis of the advantages and disadvantages of both approaches through the lens of established design principles.

Current Design: Separate AcctInfo and AcctManager

The current design employs a separation between AcctInfo, which holds account data, and AcctManager, which handles operations related to account management. This separation has several advantages:

Pros

1. **Separation of Concerns**: The adherence to the Single Responsibility Principle (SRP) is one of the most significant benefits of this approach. By maintaining distinct classes for data management (AcctInfo) and operational logic (AcctManager), each class can focus on a single aspect of functionality, reducing the risk of unintended interactions that can lead to bugs.

2. **Reusability**: The separation enhances code reusability. AcctInfo can be utilized across various parts of the application without being tied to the operational logic in AcctManager. This modularity

allows for the development of other systems that can incorporate AcctInfo independently, thus broadening its applicability.

3. **Easier Maintenance**: When changes are necessary, the impact on the overall system is minimized. Modifications to account operations can be isolated within AcctManager without affecting AcctInfo. This clear delineation simplifies debugging and facilitates updates, as developers can focus on specific components.

Cons

1. **Greater Complexity**: While the separation of concerns is beneficial, it can introduce unnecessary complexity. The introduction of multiple classes for closely related functionalities may require additional classes and methods, complicating the overall architecture of the system.

2. **Closer Interconnection**: Despite the intended separation, there may still be a strong interdependence between AcctInfo and AcctManager. Frequent interactions between these components can lead to tighter coupling, which can negate some of the benefits of having separate classes.

Combined Design: Single Account Object

An alternative approach involves merging AcctInfo and AcctManager into a single Account object. This design offers its own set of advantages and disadvantages:

Pros

1. **Streamlined Structure**: The combination of AcctInfo and AcctManager into one Account object simplifies the overall architecture of the ATM system. This reduction in the number of classes can

decrease the complexity of interactions, making the system easier to understand.

2. **Unified Representation**: By consolidating both data and functionality, the Account object provides a cohesive representation of account information and its associated operations. This can lead to more intuitive use of the object in various contexts.

3. **Reliability**: With a single object managing both data and operations, the consistency of the system is enhanced. Changes to account information and operational logic are contained within one object, reducing the likelihood of discrepancies.

Cons

1. **Violation of SRP**: A significant drawback of this design is the potential violation of the Single Responsibility Principle. By combining data and

behavior in one class, the Account object may end up having multiple responsibilities, which can lead to difficulties in understanding and managing the code.

2. **Reduced Reusability**: The merged Account object can limit reusability. In scenarios where only the account data or the operational logic is needed, the combined object becomes less flexible, complicating its use in different contexts.

3. **Complex Changes**: Modifications to the Account class can become more complicated, as any changes must consider both data and operational aspects. This complexity increases the potential for errors during development and maintenance.

Design Principles Employed

The analysis of these two design approaches is framed by several key software design principles, particularly the Single Responsibility Principle (SRP) and encapsulation.

- **Single Responsibility Principle (SRP)**: This principle emphasizes that a class should have only one reason to change. The separation of AcctInfo and AcctManager upholds this principle, allowing for distinct areas of responsibility. Conversely, the combined design risks breaching SRP by merging functionalities that should remain distinct.

- **Encapsulation**: Both designs can achieve encapsulation, but the approach differs. The separate design encapsulates data and operations within distinct classes, whereas the combined design centralizes these elements within a single object. This shift has implications for how easily data and methods can be accessed and modified.

- **Coupling and Cohesion**: The separate design promotes low coupling, which is beneficial for maintainability, but may reduce cohesion since related operations are distributed across classes. In contrast, the combined design may exhibit higher cohesion due to the integration of related functionalities but risks tighter coupling, which can lead to challenges in system scalability and adaptability.

Conclusion

The analysis of the design approaches for the ATM system illustrates the complexity inherent in software design decisions. Both the separate and combined designs present distinct advantages and disadvantages that must be weighed against the specific needs of the system.

If the ATM system anticipates frequent interactions between data and operations, merging AcctInfo and

AcctManager could simplify the architecture and enhance usability. However, if prioritizing separation of concerns and reusability is essential, maintaining distinct classes is the more prudent choice. Ultimately, the design should strive for a balance between simplicity, maintainability, and adherence to established design principles.

Chapter 8: Software Reengineering and Documentation

Introduction

In the rapidly evolving field of software development, the need for effective management of legacy systems and the creation of comprehensive documentation is paramount. This chapter delves into the concepts of software reengineering and documentation, highlighting their significance in maintaining and enhancing software applications over time. By exploring the principles of reverse engineering and the various forms of documentation, this discussion aims to provide a foundational understanding crucial for software practitioners.

Software Reengineering

Software reengineering is a vital process that involves examining and altering existing software systems to improve their functionality, maintainability, and performance. This is particularly essential when dealing with legacy systems, which may no longer meet current operational requirements or technological standards.

Reverse Engineering

A key component of software reengineering is reverse engineering, which entails deconstructing a system to understand its components and functionality. This process is critical for several reasons:

1. **Assessment of Legacy Systems**: Before reengineering can occur, understanding the existing system is essential. Reverse engineering allows developers to identify outdated features, performance bottlenecks, and areas for improvement.

2. **Platform Upgrades**: As technology advances, legacy systems often require updates to function effectively on modern platforms. Reverse engineering helps ensure that these systems can be integrated with new technologies, enhancing their capabilities without a complete rewrite.

3. **Feature Integration**: Through reverse engineering, developers can assess which new features would add value to a legacy system. This insight informs the reengineering process, allowing for the strategic enhancement of software.

Program Modularization

Program modularization is another critical aspect of software reengineering. By breaking down complex systems into smaller, manageable modules, developers can enhance maintainability and scalability. The benefits of modularization include:

- **Improved Maintainability**: Smaller, focused modules are easier to understand, test, and modify, reducing the complexity associated with large monolithic applications.

- **Reusability**: Modular components can be reused across different projects, saving time and effort in future development.

- **Facilitated Testing**: With modularization, testing can be performed on individual components, making it easier to identify and fix bugs.

Software Documentation

Effective documentation is fundamental to the software development lifecycle. It serves as a guide for developers, stakeholders, and end users, ensuring that systems can be understood and maintained efficiently.

Types of Documentation

Software documentation can be categorized into two primary forms: process documentation and product documentation.

1. **Process Documentation**: This type outlines the methodologies and practices used during the software development process. It includes information about project planning, design decisions, coding standards, and testing procedures. Process documentation is essential for maintaining consistency and quality across software projects.

2. **Product Documentation**: Product documentation focuses on the software itself, detailing its features, functionalities, and usage instructions. This includes user manuals, API documentation, and system architecture descriptions. Clear and concise product documentation ensures that users can effectively

interact with the software, minimizing confusion and support requests.

Importance of Clarity and Conciseness

One of the key takeaways from studying software documentation is the necessity for clarity and conciseness. Documentation should provide enough detail to be informative without overwhelming the reader. Striking this balance is crucial:

- **Avoiding Overly Lengthy Documents**: While thorough documentation is important, excessive length can lead to difficulties in navigation and comprehension. Developers should aim to create documents that are detailed yet easily modifiable, facilitating updates without extensive rewrites.

- **Enhancing Usability**: Clear documentation enhances user experience, making it easier for colleagues and end users to understand and utilize the software effectively.

Application of Ideas and Concepts

The principles of software reengineering and documentation are not only theoretical but also highly applicable in practical scenarios. As I engage with software development projects, I intend to incorporate these principles by:

- **Implementing Reengineering Techniques**: I will apply reengineering strategies when dealing with legacy systems, ensuring they are updated for modern use while integrating new features that enhance functionality.

- **Emphasizing Modularization**: Adopting modularization practices will allow me to develop maintainable and scalable applications, ultimately improving the quality of my code.

- **Focusing on Documentation Quality**: By prioritizing the creation of clear and useful documentation, I aim to produce resources that benefit both my development team and the end users, ensuring a smooth interaction with the software.

Important Reflection

Reflecting on the concepts of software reengineering and documentation has underscored the importance of balance in software development. The need to maintain thoroughness in documentation while ensuring it remains easy to modify has become a central consideration for me. This realization prompts a reevaluation of my approach to documentation in my projects, driving me to prioritize clarity and utility to fulfill its intended purpose without complicating software maintenance.

Conclusion

Software reengineering and documentation are integral components of successful software development. By understanding the principles of reverse engineering, program modularization, and effective documentation practices, developers can enhance the longevity and usability of software systems. As technology continues to evolve, the importance of these concepts will only increase, making them essential knowledge for anyone involved in software development.

Chapter 9: Conclusion

As we conclude this exploration of software engineering principles and practices, we reflect on the key insights gained from Chapters 1 through 8. Each chapter has contributed to a comprehensive understanding of the multifaceted aspects of software development, emphasizing the importance of both technical skills and thoughtful design.

Chapter Summaries

Chapter 1 introduced the foundational concepts of software engineering, highlighting the significance of systematic approaches to software development. We discussed the software lifecycle, including the stages of planning, design, implementation, and maintenance, underscoring the importance of each phase in delivering high-quality software.

Chapter 2 delved into software requirements, emphasizing the necessity of gathering and analyzing user needs. This chapter reinforced that understanding the end user's perspective is crucial for developing software that meets real-world demands. We explored techniques for effective requirements gathering, ensuring that software solutions are both relevant and functional.

Chapter 3 focused on software design principles, including modularity, abstraction, and encapsulation. We examined design patterns and their role in creating flexible and maintainable software architectures. The chapter illustrated how good design practices can significantly impact the ease of software evolution and adaptability to change.

Chapter 4 explored various programming paradigms, such as procedural, object-oriented, and functional programming. Understanding these paradigms allowed us to appreciate the diverse approaches available to developers, enabling the selection of the most suitable methodology for specific projects and challenges.

Chapter 5 highlighted the importance of testing and quality assurance in software development. We discussed different testing methodologies, including unit, integration, and system testing, and emphasized that thorough testing is essential to ensure software reliability and user satisfaction.

Chapter 6 examined the role of software project management, emphasizing the need for effective planning, monitoring, and communication throughout the development process. We explored methodologies like Agile and Waterfall, illustrating how choosing the right project management approach can influence the success of software projects.

Chapter 7 focused on the concepts of software reengineering and documentation. We learned about reverse engineering as a tool for understanding legacy systems and the importance of clear, concise documentation in facilitating both development and user interaction. This chapter underscored the need for balancing thoroughness with maintainability in documentation practices.

Chapter 8 further emphasized the principles of reengineering and the significance of maintaining software over time. We explored modularization as a means to enhance maintainability and the necessity of robust documentation for ensuring long-term software usability. The insights gained here are crucial for navigating the challenges of evolving software landscapes.

Final Reflections

Collectively, these chapters provide a holistic view of software engineering, emphasizing the interconnectedness of design, development, testing, and documentation. As we navigate the complexities of software projects, it is essential to apply the principles learned throughout this journey. By prioritizing user needs, adhering to design best practices, and maintaining clear documentation, software developers can create robust, adaptable, and user-friendly applications.

The field of software engineering is continuously evolving, driven by technological advancements and changing user expectations. By remaining committed to lifelong learning and applying these foundational principles, we can not only meet the challenges of today but also contribute to the future of software development in meaningful ways.

Bibliography

Aldrich, J., & Garrod, C. (2015). Assigning Responsibilities. In *Principles of Software Construction: Objects, Design and Concurrency*. Institute for Software Research. Retrieved from https://www.cs.cmu.edu/~charlie/courses/15-214/2015-fall/slides/03b-assigning-responsibilities.pdf

Ambler, S. (2003-2018). UML 2 Use Case Diagrams: An Agile Introduction. *Agile Modeling*. Retrieved from http://www.agilemodeling.com/artifacts/useCaseDiagram.htm

Bentley, J. E. (n.d.). Software Testing Fundamentals— Concepts, Roles, and Terminology. SAS Institute Inc. Retrieved from http://www2.sas.com/proceedings/sugi30/141-30.pdf

Bunus, P. (n.d.). FDA149 Software Engineering Design Patterns Examples. Linköping University Institute of

Technology. http://www.ida.liu.se/~chrke55/courses/SWE/bunus/DP02_1slide.pdf

Jackson, D., & Devadas, S. (2005). 6.170 Laboratory in Software Engineering. Massachusetts Institute of Technology: MIT OpenCourseWare. Retrieved from https://ocw.mit.edu/courses/electrical-engineering-and-computer-science/6-170-laboratory-in-software-engineering-fall-2005/lecture-notes/lec18.pdf

Jackson, M. (2004). Problem Frames and Software Engineering. The Open University. Retrieved from https://people.csail.mit.edu/dnj/teaching/6898/lecture-notes/session8/slides/mj-problem-frames.pdf

Jackson, M. (2006). Problem Frames - A Lecture [Presentation slides]. Massachusetts Institute of Technology. Retrieved from http://people.csail.mit.edu/dnj/teaching/6898/lecture-notes/session8/slides/mj-problem-frames.pdf

Marchese, F. T. (2013, March 15). How to Make a Domain Model Tutorial. In Lecture 8, Chapter 8 Software Testing. Pace University. Retrieved from http://csis.pace.edu/~marchese/CS389/L8/DomainModel-UML_short.pdf

Marsic, I. (2012). Software Engineering. Rutgers: The State University of New Jersey. Retrieved from https://my.uopeople.edu/pluginfile.php/57436/mod_book/chapter/46513/CS4403MarsicTextbook.pdf

McCabe, T. J. (1976). A Complexity Measure. *IEEE Transactions on Software Engineering*, 2(4), 308-320. Retrieved from http://www.literateprogramming.com/mccabe.pdf

Sommerville, I. (2000). Software Reengineering. Retrieved from https://my.uopeople.edu/pluginfile.php/1861763/mod_book/chapter/512143/SWReeng.pdf

Sommerville, I. (2004). Chapter 26: Software Cost Estimation. In *Software Engineering 7* (pp. 612-640). Pearson Education Ltd. Retrieved from https://ifs.host.cs.st-andrews.ac.uk/Books/SE7/SampleChapters/ch26.pdf

Sommerville, I. (2010). Chapter 30: Documentation. Retrieved from https://ifs.host.cs.st-andrews.ac.uk/Books/SE9/WebChapters/PDF/Ch_30%20Documentation.pdf

Introduction to Software Engineering/Architecture/Design Patterns. (n.d.). *Wikibooks*. Retrieved from https://en.wikibooks.org/wiki/Introduction_to_Software_Engineering/Architecture/Design_Patterns

Watson, A. H., & McCabe, T. J. (1996). Structured Testing: A Testing Methodology Using the Cyclomatic Complexity Metric. In D. Wallace (Ed.), *NIST Special Publication 500-235*. McCabe Software. Retrieved from www.mccabe.com/pdf/mccabe-nist235r.pdf